WHISPER

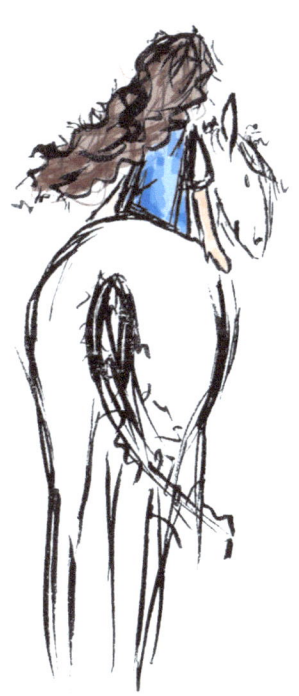

Becky Loosemore

Copyright © 2023 Becky Loosemore

All rights reserved. No part of this book may be reproduced
or used in any manner without the prior written permission of the copyright owner

ISBN 978-1-3999-4618-6

First paperback published: February 2023

For Fraser.

The little girl sits quietly by herself. She feels very lonely and would like to make some friends.

But she cannot speak aloud.

She speaks in her head, but the words just will not come out.

Each day she watches the other children playing, wishing she could play too, but without her voice she is worried what they will think of her.

She is starting school tomorrow and is feeling very nervous about it.

Whilst watching the other children play, the little girl sees something different in the distance.

"What is that?" she thinks to herself.

It's a white horse.

"I wonder why that little girl is sitting all alone," said the white horse to himself.

"She looks so sad."

So he trotted over to investigate.

"Hello" said the white horse.

He made her jump,

but to her surprise,

she whispered "Hello" back.

"Would you like some company?" asked the white horse.

"Yes" she whispered again.

"Why do you look so sad?"

"I start school tomorrow," whispered the little girl.

"I am so nervous. What if nobody wants to be my friend?"

"There's no need to be nervous," replied the horse.

"You can make friends. The important thing is to always be yourself and be kind to others."

The next day she started school.

When the teacher asked her to introduce herself, she froze and couldn't say a word.

Her voice was trapped again.

The other children did not understand why she could not speak. They played happily together, but the little girl did not join in.

"Why am I not like the other children?" she thought sadly to herself.

She walked home alone.

All she wanted was to see the white horse again.

"I could not speak," whispered the little girl.

"They wanted me to talk, but my voice would not come out. Nobody understands. How can I make friends if I cannot talk."

"Give them time," replied the horse. "You do not have to speak if you do not want to."

"How about we have some fun?" suggested the horse.

The little girl was nervous, but trusting the horse, she climbed up on his back and they galloped across the fields.

"I believe you have many wonderful things to say," said the white horse.

"But if you choose not to, that is okay too. You can always listen."

"You can learn many great things by listening" explained the white horse.

"But what if the other children won't play with me if I don't speak?" asked the little girl.

"You do not have to speak until you are ready. Until then, I will be here for you," said the horse.

"Why don't you come and meet me before school tomorrow and I will see if I can help" suggested the horse.

As the teacher waited at the school gates for the children to arrive, she was in for a big surprise.

"Who is this?" the teacher said.

"My friend" spoke the little girl.

CPSIA information can be obtained
at www.ICGtesting.com
Printed in the USA
LVHW010721050723
751506LV00004BA/18